Getting into Cricket

Ron Thomas and Joe Herran

MACMILLAN
LIBRARY

First published in 2005 by
MACMILLAN EDUCATION AUSTRALIA PTY LTD
627 Chapel Street, South Yarra 3141

Visit our website at www.macmillan.com.au

Associated companies and representatives throughout the world.

National Library of Australia
Cataloguing-in-Publication data

Thomas, Ron, 1947–.
  Cricket.

  Includes index.
  For middle primary school students.
  ISBN 0 7329 9707 0.

  1. Cricket – Juvenile literature. I. Herran, Joe. II.
  Title. (Series: Thomas, Ron, 1947– Getting into).

796.358

Edited by Helena Newton
Text and cover design by Cristina Neri, Canary Graphic Design
Illustrations by Nives Porcellato and Andy Craig
Photo research by Legend Images

Printed in China

Acknowledgements
The authors wish to acknowledge and thank Sam and Ray Leetham for their
assistance and advice in the writing of this book.

The authors and the publisher are grateful to the following for permission to
reproduce copyright material:

Cover photographs: Cricket ball courtesy of Photodisc, and player courtesy of Clive
Rose/Getty Images

Australian Picture Library/Empics, p. 6 (bottom); Getty Images, p. 23; Arif Ali/AFP/
Getty Images, p. 27; Daniel Berehulak/Getty Images, pp. 22, 29; Laurence Griffiths/
ALLSPORT/Getty Images, p. 24; Nick Laham/Getty Images, p. 5; Stephen Munday
/Allsport/Getty Images, p. 30; Clive Rose/Getty Images, pp. 4, 28; Dean Treml/AFP/
Getty Images, p. 7 (bottom); Greg Wood/AFP/Getty Images, p. 26; Photodisc, pp. 1,
6 (top), 7 (top).

While every care has been taken to trace and acknowledge copyright, the publisher
tenders their apologies for any accidental infringement where copyright has proved
untraceable. Where the attempt has been unsuccessful, the publisher welcomes
information that would redress the situation.

Contents

Glossary words

When a word is printed in **bold**, you can look up its meaning in the Glossary on page 31.

The game

Cricket is popular with young and older people who play in local, district and state teams. An indoor version of cricket, played by teams of eight, is popular too.

International cricket is governed by the International Cricket Council (ICC). International women's cricket is governed by the International Women's Cricket Council (IWCC). These bodies aim to develop the game of cricket and make it commercially successful, while maintaining its traditions. International cricket is played in England, Australia, West Indies, South Africa, India, Pakistan, New Zealand, Sri Lanka, Bangladesh and Zimbabwe. Millions of supporters attend five-day test matches and one-day games played by professional cricketers.

England playing New Zealand in Leeds, England, during the 2004 test series

Did you know?

In the early days of cricket there was no rule about how wide the bat should be. One batter used a bat almost 30 centimetres wide and couldn't be bowled out because his bat was as wide as the wicket.

The history of cricket

Cricket-like games, called club ball and stool ball, were played in England more than 500 years ago. In club ball, a batter used a stick or pole to hit the leather-covered ball. In stool ball, a stool was used as a **wicket**. The bowler tried to hit the stool with the ball and the 'batter' hit the ball using a bare hand.

Playing a match

Cricket is played between two 11-player teams. Two umpires, one at each end of the **pitch**, control the game. The game begins with a coin toss and the winning captain chooses to bat or field. Two batters defend their wickets against the fielding team's bowlers. When one batter hits the ball, each batter runs to the opposite wicket to score a **run**. If the batter hits the ball to the boundary, a **four** is scored, meaning four runs are scored without running. A **six** is scored if the ball goes over the boundary without touching the ground.

The bowler bowls a series of six fair or legal deliveries, called an **over**. The bowler and fielders try to get the batters out by knocking down the wicket or catching a hit ball. The wicket-keeper can knock down a stump or bail with the ball to get the batter out. A batter is also out if the ball hits their pads while they are in front of their stumps. When a batter goes out, another player takes their place. This continues until ten batters are out, which is the end of an **innings**. Then the opposing team has its innings. The team that scores the most runs wins.

A test match is a match that can last for five days. Each side plays two innings of more than 90 overs each. One-day matches last for about eight hours and each team has one innings of about 50 overs each. Short games of an hour or two are also played.

Indian captain Sourav Ganguly tosses the coin before the 2003 World Cup final against Australia.

Equipment

Equipment such as bats, balls and wickets used in competition must all meet the standards set by the sport's governing body. All of the balls used in matches must be approved by the umpires and captains before the match begins.

Cricket balls and bats

Balls are round and measure between 22.4 and 22.9 centimetres around. They are made of cork, bound with twine. The casing is red leather with a seam of stitching around the middle. White balls are used for night games played under lights. Balls weigh between 115.9 and 163 grams.

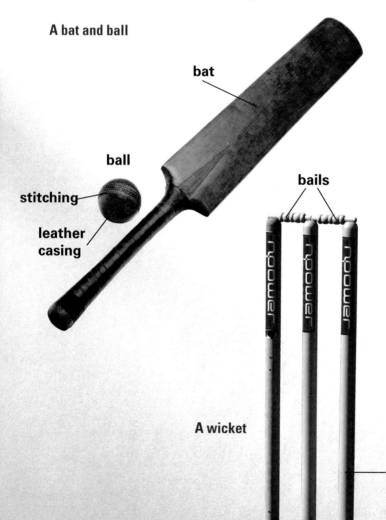

A bat and ball

bat

ball

stitching

leather casing

bails

A wicket

stumps

Bats are usually made of willow and are no longer than 96.5 centimetres and no wider than 10.8 centimetres. Junior cricketers use shorter, narrower bats.

Wickets

Wickets are made up of three wooden stumps with two wooden bails across the top. There is one wicket at each end of the pitch. Stumps are 71.1 centimetres high and the two bails are each 11.1 centimetres long.

Clothing

It is a tradition that cricketers wear all-white clothing. Men wear shirts and trousers. Women wear shirts and either trousers or skirts. Coloured clothing can be worn for one-day matches.

helmet with face mask

Batting pads

Batting pads are strapped to the batter's legs for protection. Padding may also be worn under clothing to protect other parts of the batter's body from hard cricket balls.

Batting gloves

Padded batting gloves protect the batter's hands.

batting gloves

batting pads

Head protection

A helmet fitted with a face mask protects the batter from injury. Players fielding close to the batter may also wear helmets. Players wear caps or visors to protect them from the sun.

spiked cricket shoes

Shoes and socks

Cricket shoes have spiked soles and heels to stop players from slipping on the field. Cotton or woollen socks absorb sweat and keep a player's feet comfortable.

Wicket-keepers' pads are shorter than batting pads. The wicket-keeper also wears protective gloves.

The playing field

Cricket is played on a grass field that is usually oval-shaped but can be any shape. The field is usually marked with a boundary.

The pitch

The pitch is the rectangular strip between the wickets. A grass pitch is rolled and mown before the game. It is covered during a match if it rains. The **popping crease** marks the border between safe and unsafe territory for running batters. The **bowling crease** is the line which the bowler stands behind. Part of the foot needs to be behind this crease when bowling. The **return crease** is the line that the bowler cannot step outside when bowling.

A cricket pitch

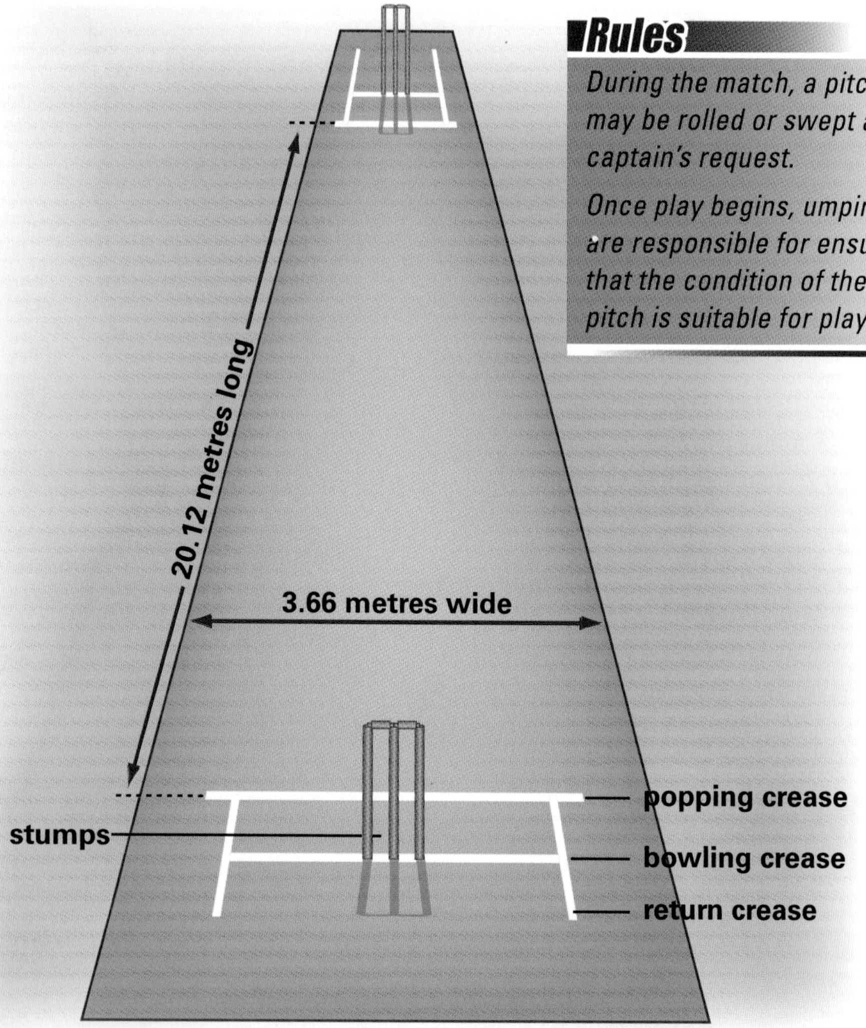

20.12 metres long

3.66 metres wide

stumps

popping crease

bowling crease

return crease

Rules

During the match, a pitch may be rolled or swept at a captain's request.

Once play begins, umpires are responsible for ensuring that the condition of the pitch is suitable for play.

The players

The batters from the batting team defend their wickets against the 11 players of the bowling and fielding side. The striker is the batter who is facing the bowler and the non-striker is the batter at the opposite end of the pitch.

Fielding positions

Fielding positions are decided by the captain and the bowler. They are changed after each over depending on:

- the end from which the bowler is bowling
- whether the bowler is a fast or slow bowler
- whether the batter is left- or right-handed.

The possible fielders', umpires' and batters' positions

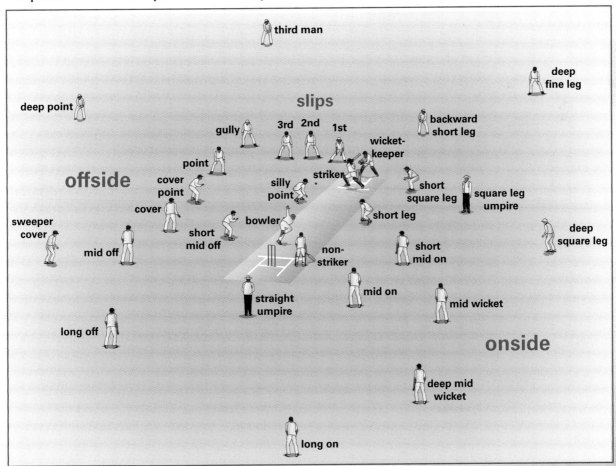

Skills

Beginning players learn the basic skills of cricket, such as batting, bowling and fielding, which includes throwing and catching the ball, and wicket-keeping. With practice, players will develop these skills and improve their performance.

Batting

To bat well the batter needs to have a good grip on the bat, a comfortable stance and smooth backlift before hitting the ball.

Grip

To grip the bat, the hands are close together at the top of the handle with fingers and thumbs wrapped around it. The thumb and first finger on each hand form V shapes down the bat.

Stance

In the batting stance, the batter's feet are shoulder-width apart, side-on to the bowler, and the weight is over the balls of the feet. Knees are slightly bent and the batter looks over the front shoulder. The bat rests behind the back foot.

Backlift

The correct grip, stance and backlift

For every shot, the batter lifts the bat back smoothly. The backlift starts as the bowler's arm starts its upward swing.

The batter needs to have a good grip on the bat.

In the batting stance, the weight is balanced and the batter looks towards the bowler.

The backlift is smooth and the bat lifted straight back.

Playing a shot

The batter must decide quickly how to play each ball. If the ball **length** is short, and the ball bounces a long way in front of the player, the batter steps back to play it. If the ball is fuller and bounces near the batter, the batter steps forward to play the shot. For a ball that bounces in between a short- and a full-length ball, the batter can play either forward or back.

Batting shots are either attacking shots used to score runs, or defensive 'stopping' shots used to stop the ball and defend the wicket.

Attacking shots

The drive

The drive is an attacking shot. The batter steps forward and sideways to the ball with knees bent and head down. The shoulders point in the direction the batter intends to hit the ball. The backlift goes over the stumps and, after hitting the ball, the batter swings the bat and follows through past the body.

The straight drive is a forward drive down the centre of the pitch. Backlift is over the stumps. The batter's head, shoulder and front foot point down the pitch.

The cover drive is played to a full-length ball. The front foot points in the direction the ball is to go and weight is transferred from the back foot to the front foot. The backlift is high and the batter strikes the ball with a full swing.

The straight drive

1 The bat is lifted up behind the head.

2 The batter leans forward with the head over the front shoulder.

3 The bat is pulled straight down and grazes the inside of the front foot.

4 The bottom hand lifts the bat upwards as the shot is followed through.

The sweep

The sweep is another attacking shot. The batter plays the sweep to a good length ball and finishes on one knee. The bat sweeps horizontally round the body.

The sweep

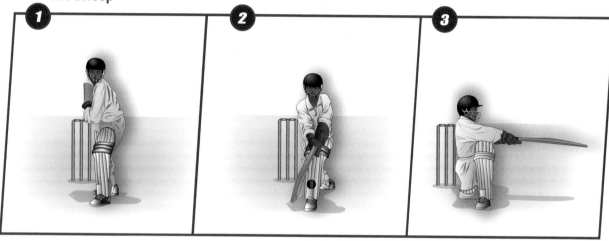

Pull shot

The pull shot is an attacking shot played to a short-pitched ball that bounces a long way in front of the batter. The batter steps onto the back foot and lifts the bat back behind the shoulder. With the body facing down the pitch, the batter hits the ball at arm's length and with a full swing.

The pull shot

Hook shot

The hook shot is an attacking shot played to a short-pitched, fast and high ball. The batter steps back and hooks the ball away. This is a dangerous shot! Missing it could mean that the ball hits the batter's helmet or face.

The hook shot

Square cut

The square cut is an attacking shot played to a short-length ball.
For the square cut, the batter moves the weight onto the back foot.
The bat is held high and is swept down to hit the ball at arm's length.

The square cut shot

Defensive shots

Defensive shots are used to stop the ball and defend the wicket, rather than to score runs.

Forward defensive shot

The forward defensive shot is used against a full-length ball. The batter steps forward and brings the bat down straight, to knock the ball to the ground.

Backward defensive shot

The backward defensive shot is used against a short-pitched ball. The batter moves the back foot towards the stumps. The bat is lifted high with the front elbow and the ball is blocked so that it drops to the ground.

The forward defensive shot

The ball is pushed forward and towards the ground for the backward defensive shot.

Bowling

Bowlers take turns, bowling a series of six legal deliveries, called an over. A bowler cannot bowl two overs in a row. Bowlers aim to:

- deliver a ball that will get the batter out
- deliver a ball that will be difficult for the batter to play
- vary the style and speed of their delivery to confuse the batter.

Grip

Bowlers grip the ball in different ways depending on the type of delivery they want to make. The basic grip is with three fingers. The first two are on either side of the seam, the thumb is under the ball and the other fingers are curled next to the ball.

The basic grip

Rule

A bowler's back foot must be inside the return crease. The front foot must not pass the popping crease. An umpire will signal a no-ball if this rule is broken.

Basic bowling action

The bowler runs up to the wicket, taking longer strides and running faster as the bowler gets closer to the **crease**. At the wicket the bowler turns sideways. The bowling arm is lifted high and the bowler's weight is on the back foot. The other arm is lowered and the bowling arm is stretched back. The bowling arm is raised high and straight and the bowler releases the ball. The bowling arm swings across the body and the shoulder of the bowling arm points down the pitch.

The basic bowling action

Line and length

The line of the ball is the path it takes after leaving the bowler's hand. A ball with good line will hit the wicket. The length of the ball is the distance the ball travels before it bounces in front of the batter. Good bowlers vary the length of the ball to confuse the batter.

Where balls of different lengths will bounce

A full toss reaches the batter without bouncing.

A yorker is a full-length ball that bounces close to the batter's feet.

A half volley is a full-length ball and the batter steps forward to play it.

A good length ball can be played forward or back.

The batter needs to step back to play a short-length ball.

A bouncer is a fast, short-length ball.

Swing and spin

Bowlers can make a ball swing or spin. Swing makes the ball travel on a curved path. Spin will cause a ball to change direction as it bounces. A swinging or spinning ball is difficult for a batter to hit.

Swing bowlers

Swing bowlers hold the ball with the seam on an angle so that it swings, or curves, while in flight. Inswing bowlers angle the seam so that the ball swings in towards the batter. The ball bounces close to the wicket. Outswing bowlers angle the seam so that the ball swings away from the batter. The bowler faces side-on as much as possible.

The inswing grip

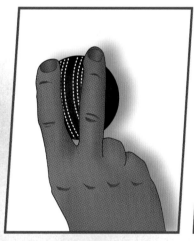

How an inswing bowl travels

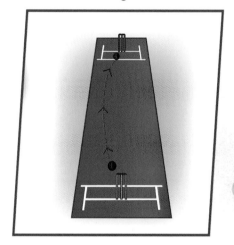

The outswing grip

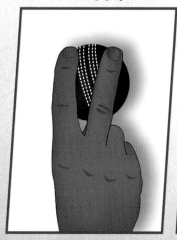
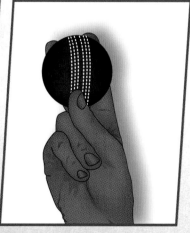

How an outswing bowl travels

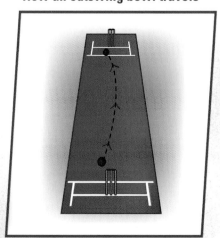

Spin bowlers

Spin bowlers turn the index finger and wrist to make the ball spin. The ball is tossed high by the bowler and changes direction after it hits the pitch.

An off-spin ball turns from the off side (in front of the batter) to the leg side (behind the batter) when bowled at a right-handed batter. The first and second fingers are spread across the top of the ball and the thumb and third finger support the ball. The first and second fingers are used to put spin on the ball and the wrist snaps forward.

An off-spin bowler

The off-spin grip

A leg-spin bowler spins the ball so that it turns from the leg side (behind the batter) to the off side (in front of the batter). As the ball is released the bowler's fingers are straightened and the third finger turns the ball clockwise. The wrist is flicked and the palm finishes facing downwards.

The leg-spin grip

A leg-spin bowler

Fielding

Fielding players aim to stop, catch and throw the ball to get the batter out. Fielding players:

- stand relaxed with their weight on the balls of the feet
- walk towards the pitch as the bowler begins the run-up
- watch the batter and the ball
- are always ready to move quickly in any direction
- can pick up a ball on the run
- can stop or catch a ball with one or two hands.

A fielder close to the wicket crouches with hands ready to take the ball.

The long barrier position

The long barrier

The long barrier is a way of stopping the ball where the fielder kneels on one knee and makes a 'long barrier' with the other knee and leg. The fingers are together and pointing downwards.

Taking a catch

Fielders cup their hands together with fingers pointing away from the body to take a catch. The elbows are away from the body and are used to cushion the impact of the catch.

Throwing

Fielders need to be able to throw powerfully, accurately and speedily. Overarm throwing is used for long throws. Underarm throws are used when the fielder is close to the wicket.

Rule

A fielding player cannot stand on or have any part of the body over the pitch while the ball is in play, until it touches the bat or the batter's body.

Wicket-keeping

The wicket-keeper needs to be ready for every ball bowled, in case the batter misses it. The wicket-keeper remains behind the wicket until the bowled ball has been touched by the batter's bat or body. The wicket-keeper must take the ball behind the stumps.

Basic stance

The wicket-keeper squats, usually about half a pace behind the wicket, with the weight on the balls of the feet. The feet are comfortably apart. The arms and gloved hands are between the knees with the palms facing the bowler. The wicket-keeper looks up and focuses on the ball.

Taking the ball

To take a ball, the wicket-keeper stands as the ball bounces and keeps the hands together as much as possible to make a large catching zone. Once the batter hits the ball, the wicket-keeper gets in behind the stumps ready for the return of the ball.

Stumped!

If a batter moves forward and outside the crease to play a ball, and the ball is missed, the wicket-keeper can catch the ball and knock the bails off the stumps. This means that the batter is out.

The basic wicket-keeping stance

As the ball bounces the wicket-keeper stands and prepares to catch it.

Rules

The game of cricket has been governed by a series of codes for over 250 years. Since it formed in 1787, the Marylebone Cricket Club (MCC) has been responsible for drawing up the code and for all changes made to it. Players need to learn and understand the basic rules before they are ready to play cricket.

Going-out rules

The batting player is out when:

- a bowled ball strikes the stumps behind the batter, causing the bails to fall
- a hit ball is caught by a fielder before it touches the ground
- the bowled ball hits the batter's hand and is caught
- a bowled ball, which would have hit the wicket, is knocked off course by any part of the batter's body, known as being out, **leg before wicket (l.b.w.).**

A batter is out when a bowled ball strikes the stumps.

A batter is out, l.b.w. when a bowled ball is knocked off course by the batter's body.

Other going-out rules

A batter is also out when:

- the batters are running between wickets, one batter is outside the batting crease and a fielding player knocks the wicket down with the ball, known as being run out

- a batter moves outside the crease while attempting to hit the ball, and the wicket-keeper catches the ball and knocks a bail off the wicket before the batting player gets the bat behind the crease, known as being stumped

- the batting wicket is knocked down with the bat or any part of the batter's body, known as being out, hit wicket

- the batter deliberately touches the ball with a hand that is not holding the bat

- the batter deliberately takes a second hit at the ball.

A wicket-keeper can get the batter out by knocking the bails off the stumps.

The batter is out when the wicket is knocked down with the bat or with any part of the batter's body.

Scoring

Batting players score one run for their team when they hit the ball and both batters run along the pitch to the opposite wicket. Runs are also scored:

- when a ball is hit and reaches or goes outside the boundary (four runs if a ball bounces or rolls to the boundary, six runs if the ball clears the boundary 'on the full' without touching the ground first, or if it goes outside the boundary)
- when a ball is lost (six runs)
- for a **no-ball**, which is a ball bowled in an illegal way, such as when the bowler's feet cross the crease or when a ball is thrown, not bowled (one run)
- for a wide ball, which is when a ball is bowled so high over, or so wide of the wicket that it is out of the reach of the batter (one run)
- for a **bye**, which is when a ball passes the batter without hitting either the bat or body and the wicket-keeper misses it
- for a **leg bye**, which includes runs taken after the ball hits the batter on a part of the body, other than the hand, without hitting the bat.

Runs scored from byes, leg byes, no-balls and wide balls are called extras or sundries.

After hitting the ball, the batting player tries to run to the end of the pitch to score a run before a member of the opposing team gets him or her out by knocking down the wicket.

Scorers

There are usually two scorers for a cricket match, one for each side. Scorers sit together and compare notes to make sure no mistakes are made. An official score book is used to record the number of runs scored as well as information about each batter's innings, such as the length of the innings, boundaries hit and how the batter went out.

The scorers also record information about bowlers, including how many overs were bowled and the number of runs scored from each over. The number of overs with no runs scored ('maiden' overs) is noted, as is the number of wickets taken during the bowler's overs.

❙Rule❙

Scorers must accept all instructions and immediately recognise all signals given by the umpires.

Scorers must watch for and respond to an umpire's signals.

Umpires

There are two umpires who stand at each end of the pitch to control the game and make decisions according to the Laws of Cricket set by the Marylebone Cricket Club (MCC). The umpires:

- check that the wickets are properly set before the match begins
- judge if play is fair or unfair (unfair actions include time-wasting by players, obstruction of a batter by a fielder, and bowling in a way intended to strike a batter)
- decide if the ground is fit and safe for play
- decide if there is enough light for play
- signal their decisions to the scorers
- wait until a signal has been answered before allowing play to continue
- check that the scoring for the match is accurate
- count the number of balls in an over and call 'over'
- answer appeals from players for 'bowled', 'caught' or 'l.b.w.' and so on
- call 'play' at the beginning of an innings and 'time' at the end of play.

Lord's cricket ground in England, home of the MCC

The ground at the MCC is known as Lord's after the founder of the club, Thomas Lord.

Umpires' signals

Umpires use a code of signals to let players and scorers know of their decisions about scoring, whether a batter is out, and all other decisions according to the rules of the game.

These are some of the signals used by cricket umpires.

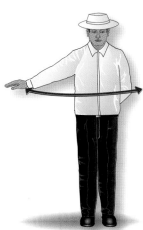

Waving one arm back and forth across the body signals a four.

Both arms held out with elbows bent and hands raised signals a six.

Holding up one finger signals that a player is out.

Touching the shoulder signals a short run, meaning both batters did not place their bats in the opposite popping crease.

One arm held out with elbow bent and hand raised signals a bye.

Touching a raised, bent knee with one hand signals a leg bye.

One arm extended to the side signals a no-ball.

Both arms extended to the sides signals a wide ball.

Appeals

If a bowler believes that the he or she has bowled a batter out, the bowler appeals 'how's that' to the umpire at the bowling end. The umpire then gives a ruling. The umpire's decision is final.

Rule

Umpires must wait until a signal has been recognised by a scorer before allowing the game to continue.

Player fitness

Cricket players need to be fit if they are to perform to the best of their ability. Running, swimming and cycling build stamina and fitness.

Warming up and stretching

Performing side and arm stretches before playing cricket helps to prevent injuries.

Before a game or a practice session, it is important for cricket players to warm up all their muscles. This helps to prevent injuries such as muscle tears, strains and joint injuries. Gentle jogging helps players to warm up. Stretching makes players more flexible and helps the muscles and joints to move easily.

Neck stretches

The player tilts the head forward and slowly rolls the head to one shoulder and then the other. These exercises help to prevent stiffness in the neck and keep the neck flexible.

Side stretches

The player raises the right hand above the head and slowly leans to the left. Then the stretch is repeated, raising the left hand above the head and leaning slowly to the right. The raised arm can also be held with the other hand to stretch the arm. Side stretches are good exercises for bowlers because bowlers need to twist and bend from the waist.

Calf stretches

The player places one foot in front of the other and leans forward, but keeps the back heel on the ground. The player pushes forward until the calf muscle in the back leg stretches. The stretch is repeated for the other leg.

Thigh stretches

Standing on one leg, the player holds the ankle of the raised leg. The player pulls the foot back to stretch the thigh, keeping the knees close together. The player can lean against a wall or hold onto another player for balance. The stretch is then repeated for the other leg.

Stretching exercises, such as thigh stretches, are done in an easy and relaxed way and each position is held for at least 10 seconds.

Back stretch

The player crouches down on all fours with the head up and back flat. Then the player tucks the head under and arches the back upwards. The player feels the stretch in the upper back.

Groin stretch

The player sits on the ground with the knees bent and pointing out to either side. Holding onto the ankles, the player pulls them gently in towards the body. The player pushes down gently on the thighs with the arms so that the legs move towards the ground.

Competition

People play and enjoy cricket at local, district and state levels. International cricket is played by men and women representing their countries.

International competition

The International Cricket Council (ICC) is the governing body for international test matches and One Day International (ODI) cricket. The four key responsibilities of the ICC are:

- to provide leadership for the development of cricket
- to promote the globalisation of cricket
- to maintain and enhance the traditional spirit of the game
- to ensure the commercial success of cricket.

Cricket World Cup

The ICC Cricket World Cup is held every four years and is the world's biggest cricket tournament. It is a series of one-day matches between teams from all the test-playing countries, as well as teams from countries that have qualified by playing in the ICC Trophy. The ICC Trophy is an event for non-test-playing countries, such as Canada and Scotland.

Fast, one-day cricket is very popular with spectators.

One-day or limited-over matches

These matches for both men and women are played in a single day and each side bats only once. Bowlers are usually limited to ten overs each.

Women's international cricket

The International Women's Cricket Council (IWCC) organises a test cricket competition between the member countries. The IWCC also stages the Women's Cricket World Cup every four years.

History of women's cricket

The first women's cricket international tour took place in 1934 to 1935 when an English team toured and played in Australia. In 1960, the first international women's test series was played between South Africa and England. In 1976, the first women's test at Lord's cricket ground was played between England and Australia.

Women's international teams, such as Australia and New Zealand, also play one-day matches.

Test matches

Test matches are those matches played between teams of the ten official test nations, England, Australia, West Indies, South Africa, India, Pakistan, New Zealand, Sri Lanka, Bangladesh and Zimbabwe. Teams from two countries play matches lasting for a maximum of five days and both sides get the opportunity to bat twice.

History of the Ashes

Test matches between Australia and England are famous test series matches and are known as 'Ashes' tests. In 1882, England lost to a touring Australian side. This defeat was written about in a newspaper as 'the death of English cricket'. As a joke, some cricket bails were burnt and the ashes placed in a small urn. The urn was presented to the Australian team and taken back as a trophy.

Did you know?

The highest score in a test match was by Sri Lanka against India in 1997. Sri Lanka scored 952 for 6.

Cricket teams still play to win the 'Ashes', but the winner receives a modern glass trophy, rather than the original Ashes urn.

Glossary

bowling crease the line which the bowler stands behind to deliver the ball; part of the bowler's foot must stay behind this crease

bye an extra run scored after the ball passes the striker, or current batter, without hitting either the bat or the body

crease one of the white lines marked on the pitch to show different areas of play, including the bowling crease, popping crease and return crease

four four runs scored by hitting the ball to the boundary rather than by running

innings the period in which one team bats, trying to score as many runs as possible

leg before wicket (l.b.w.) a batter is out, l.b.w. if a ball that hits the batter would have otherwise hit the wicket

leg bye a run scored after the ball strikes part of the current batter's body, other than the hand

length the distance along the pitch from the bowler to where the ball bounces

no-ball an illegal bowling delivery because the bowler stepped outside the crease

over six legal balls bowled by a bowler in a row

pitch the area between the bowling creases along which the batting players run and the bowler bowls

popping crease the white line marked on the pitch in front of each wicket, marking the border between safe and unsafe territory for the batters when they take runs

return crease the lines marking the places on either side of the bowler that the bowler cannot step outside of when bowling

run a score made when both batters run from one popping crease to the other

six six runs scored by hitting the ball over the boundary without touching the ground

stumped to get the batter out by knocking down a stump or removing a bail using the ball in one hand

wicket a frame made up of three stumps with two bails across the top, which the bowler aims at; also, the area between the two wickets at either end of the pitch

Index